Cracking the High-Performance Team Code

Action Steps for

Building Turbocharged Teams

Dana Borowka, MA & Ellen Borowka, MA

www.lighthouseconsulting.com

ISBN-10: 1985582341

ISBN-13: 978-1985582347

Cover illustration by Warren Gebert, IllustrationSource.com

LIGHTHOUSE PUBLISHING

3130 Wilshire Blvd., Suite 550

Santa Monica, CA 90403

Contents

Foreword from Sam Reese, CEO of Vistage International

This book contains excellent advice from Vistage Chairs and Vistage speakers who have worked with companies all over the globe to help their leaders build high-performing teams.

Building high-performance teams is central to the success of every leader. Decisions related to this endeavor are often the most important decisions leaders face. Vistage's sole purpose is to help high-integrity leaders make great decisions that benefit their companies, families and communities.

Founded in 1957, Vistage facilitates private advisory groups for CEOs, senior executives and business owners. An exclusive community of more than 22,000 business leaders across a broad array of industries and in twenty countries, Vistage allows members to tap into different perspectives to solve challenges, evaluate opportunities and develop strategies for better business performance.

Our vision at Vistage is to be the world's most trusted advisors to CEOs and key executives to help them become more effective leaders, and this vision is only realized if our members achieve stellar results.

An analysis of Dun and Bradstreet data revealed that Vistage members grow their companies at more than twice the rate of comparable sized nonmember companies.

Vistage groups are led by successful independent leaders, called Chairs, who provide valuable professional insight, executive coaching and serve as a guide to help members access other elements of the Vistage Platform, the world's most comprehensive decision support system for business leaders. Chairs are accomplished executives and former business owners who combine their experience, their desire to help others, and their extensive training in Vistage methodologies to help their members succeed.

Vistage members place a high value on the stable of nearly 1,000 curated speakers who regularly help members to optimize their instincts, judgment and decision making, leading to lasting results.

Thanks, Dana and Ellen Borowka, for gathering this valuable information (and thanks, Dana, for being a Vistage member and speaker for over twenty years). My hope is this book will bring clarity to CEOs, senior executives, and business owners.

Part I

The Challenge

Chapter 1

Why Cracking the Team-Building Code is Vital

The days of seat-of-the-pants leadership are over. When managers understand what really makes their people tick, they can create more productive teams. Knowing the personality traits of team members can help with motivating teams, communicating change, and delegating authority. Any business that wants to maximize productivity should be concerned with building a great team.

Take a Lesson from the Sports World

Building a great team does not just happen. Also, it is not a matter of finding the most stars to be on the team. In the world of sports, championships are frequently won by teams that do not have the most star players.

For example, UCLA's college basketball program has the international reputation of being Number 1. There is a major reason for that: his name was Coach John Wooden. Under Wooden, UCLA won an unprecedented ten NCAA championships—seven consecutively from 1966 to 1973. The stars who played for Wooden included Bill Walton and Kareem Abdul-Jabbar. But Wooden once said, "The main ingredient of stardom is the rest of the team."

By acclamation, according to the *NBA Encyclopedia*, Michael Jordan is the greatest basketball star of all time. A brief listing of his top accomplishments would include being five-time NBA MVP and six-time NBA champion. Commenting on team building, Jordan said, "Talent wins games, but teamwork and intelligence win championships."

The NFL trophy for the Super Bowl is named for Vince Lombardi, the coach who led the Green Bay Packers to five championships. It was Lombardi who said, "Individual commitment to a group effort—that is what makes a team work, a company work, a society work, a civilization work."

Championship-winning teams go all the way because the individuals do a better job of playing together as a team. Teamwork matters, both on the playing field and in the business arena.

Some Say Teamwork is Overrated

Is team building overrated? Not everyone in business today agrees with the sports analogy. Some critics of team building such as Gavin McInnes, who gave a TED talk on the subject, will paraphrase the icon of innovation, the late Steve Jobs of Apple, to make their case:

> Here's to the crazy ones, the misfits, the rebels, the troublemakers, the round pegs in the square holes...the ones who see things differently—they're not fond of rules.... You can quote them, disagree with them, glorify or vilify them, but the only thing you can't do is ignore them because they change things.... They push the human race forward, and while some may see them as the crazy ones, we see genius, because the ones who are crazy enough to think that they can change the world are the ones who do.

These critics cite many academic studies examining people's performance in groups. Far from finding a huge boost to performance from teamwork, they say the studies are neutral or only show small benefits. To make their point they quote findings such as the following:

- High-performing groups are not normal.
- Team brainstorming produces groupthink.
- Groups often have huge variations in ability from top to bottom.
- People in groups often waste time squabbling over goals.
- Groups frequently suffer downward performance spirals.

(Source: http://www.spring.org.uk/2012/03/why-teamwork-is-overrated.php)

In her book, *Quiet: The Power of Introverts in a World That Can't Stop Talking*, author Susan Cain commented upon the research by stating, "Top performers overwhelmingly worked for companies that gave their workers the most privacy, personal space, and control over their physical environments and freedom from interruption."

"Collectivism is a virus that has infected everything we do," stated McInnes in an article for the online Taki's Magazine. "I'm presently trying to get my kids into better schools and I've noticed the administrators fall into two categories: those who encourage the individual and those who think teamwork trumps personal development. Only incompetent people love the team, and they love it because it makes it harder to discover their incompetence."

(Source: http://takimag.com/article/teamwork_is_overrated_gavin_mcinnes)

As harsh as his incompetence comments are, the views of McInnes reflect what many skeptics feel about the overimportance bestowed upon team building.

Underestimating Teamwork is a Miscalculated View

However, rejecting team building because there are many who thrive working in isolation is a gross miscalculation. Critics ignore the volumes of research that prove the value of teamwork and team building.

"Team building has a bad rap," said Forbes.com columnist Brian Scudamore (March 9, 2016). "In most companies when a supervisor says, 'We're going to do some team building!' employees start re-running old episodes of The Office. It's one thing to see it on TV, but getting a real-life taste of your manager mimicking Steve Carell's insanely-awkward-try-hard leadership style just isn't as funny."

Scudamore, a branding and culture expert, says "Team building is the most important investment you can make for your people. It builds trust, mitigates conflict, encourages communication, and increases collaboration. Effective team building means more engaged employees, which is good for company culture and boosting the bottom line."

But Not All Team Building is Created Equal

Building a culture of teamwork does not happen by accident or luck. To get an edge in team building requires science—namely, the science of cognitive and personality testing of the team members.

Today there are around 2,500 cognitive personality tests on the market that can be used for team building. So how do you decide which one to use? To understand how to choose from the plethora of personality tests, it is helpful to understand the origins of these instruments.

As part of the research to help America's war effort back in the 1940s, a Harvard University instructor and psychologist named Raymond Cattell working in the Adjutant General's office devised psychological tests for the military. After World War II he accepted a research professorship at the University of Illinois where the college was developing the first electronic computer, the Illiac I, which would make it possible for the first time to do large-scale factor analyses of his personality testing theories.

Cattell used an IBM sorter and the brand-new Illiac computer to perform factor analysis on 4,500 personality-related words. The result was a test to measure intelligence and to assess personality traits known as the Sixteen Personality Factor questionnaire (16PF). First published in 1949, the 16PF profiles individuals using sixteen different personality traits. Cattell's research proved that while most people have surface personality traits that can be easily observed, we also have source traits that can be discovered only by the statistical processes of factor analysis. His sixteen measures of personality are:

1. Warmth—from reserved to attentive

2. Reasoning—from concrete thinker to conceptual thinker

3. Emotional Stability—from changeable to stable

4. Dominance—from cooperative to assertive

5. Liveliness—from restrained to spontaneous

6. Rule Consciousness—from non-conforming to dutiful

7. Social Boldness—from timid to bold

8. Sensitivity—from unsentimental to sentimental

9. Vigilance—from trusting to suspicious

10. Abstractedness—from practical to imaginative

11. Privateness—from openness to discreet

12. Apprehension—from self-assured to apprehensive

13. Openness to Change—from traditional to open to change

14. Self Reliance—from affiliative to individualistic

15. Perfectionism—from tolerant to perfectionistic

16. Tension—from relaxed to tense

In 1963 W.T. Norman verified Cattell's work but felt that only five factors really shape personality: extraversion, independence, self-control, anxiety and tough-mindedness. Dubbed the "Big Five" approach, this has become the basis of many of the modern personality tests on the market today. There have been hundreds and hundreds of studies validating the approach.

Using the "Big Five" terms, here is what a manager is looking for on a spectrum of personality:

- **Extraversion**—introvert or extravert?

- **Independence**—accommodation or independence?

- **Self-Control**—lack of restraint or self-control?

- **Anxiety**—low anxiety or high anxiety?

- **Tough-Mindedness**—receptivity or tough-mindedness?

"This is a topic that's been researched to death by the field of industrial and organizational psychology," said Peter Cappelli, management professor and director of the Center for Human Resources at the Wharton School of the University of Pennsylvania, to *Inc.* magazine in August 2006. "The amazing thing is how few companies take this seriously. It's kind of mind-boggling that they would undertake such huge investments and not pay attention to what we know about how to pick out the people who are going to be the best."

"In God We Trust; All Others Bring Data"

The famous quote, "In God we trust; all others bring data;" is attributed to W. Edwards Deming, the father of modern quality management. Professor Deming was heavily involved in the economic reconstruction of Japan after the second world war.

Deming's fundamental philosophy was that data measurement and analysis were essential to attaining superior performance in every facet of business. That includes the performance of teams.

While we are staunch advocates of in-depth work style and personality testing, we admit there are limits to its power. If you meet a profiling organization that says you can decide to hire or not hire based on test data alone, please walk away. No, run away. In-depth work style and personality testing data is no silver bullet or magic potion.

The secret is to cultivate top performers through a three-step process: assess candidates with in-depth work style and personality profiling, screen candidates for behavioral tendencies, and manage teams more effectively based on behavioral styles. The goal is to base your hiring and managing decisions on the best team-building data that can be collected.

Data allows managers to graph or chart the information to visualize the dynamic nature of the team. This is helpful to team building because it allows managers to better understand how individual team members prefer to receive and give information. This is not secret data kept from the team. On the contrary, everyone on the team should gain an understanding of the strengths of the other team members and how best to communicate with them.

Insight Leads to Better Team Performance

In-depth work style and personality testing can be a valuable resource before you hire. The true value of any assessment comes in using the insights it provides. Personality assessments lend objectivity to decisions that may otherwise be largely subjective.

A proper test should reach beyond simple profiles and decipher an employee's underlying needs. This is key for team building, conflict resolution, and succession planning. Some tests only use five or eight traits to make an assessment; this is not enough. We recommend a test that utilizes the full sixteen traits to get a complete picture of the person.

Here are eight great ways to use in-depth work style and personality testing in the workplace to crack the code of team building:

1. Get the real picture when hiring team members. Naturally all job candidates for your team want to put their best foot forward during an interview. However, through an in-depth work style and personality test, you can uncover a great deal about their ability to work well with other personalities, their problem-solving abilities, their thought processes and their ability to tolerate stress. This testing gives you objective information that can help you make an informed decision about whether these candidates would be good fits for the jobs and for the team.

2. Help team members be all that they can be. Everyone has strengths and weaknesses. Find out the real truth with an objective measure. Once you pinpoint the good and the bad, then you place them in the right positions and coach them on where to improve.

3. Take me to your leaders. In-depth personality assessments gives the manager and employees a common language about how they like to interact as a team. The assessments can help you train future managers on how to get the best out of the team.

4. Know how to manage difficult team members. Face it, there will always be difficult people and flare ups on the job. Use objective in-depth work style and personality assessments to diagnose potential sources of workplace conflict. The best way to deal with a problem is to prevent it in the first place.

5. Treat team members the way they want to be treated. In today's fast-paced world of business there is little time to get to know many of your coworkers. Using in-depth work style personality assessments as the basis for team building exercises can quickly get everyone to have a healthier respect for other ways of seeing the world.

6. Make managers better team leaders. When managers understand what makes their people tick, then they can be better leaders. Knowing the work style and personality traits can help with motivating teams, communicating change and delegating authority.

7. Pick better teams. Today so much work is done by ad hoc teams that come together for a specific purpose. Before you assemble a team, it pays to know the strengths and weaknesses of the team members. Sometimes this can be the difference between a productive team that gets the job done and one that pulls apart at the seams.

8. Set up employees for success. Sometimes we hire the right employee and then give that person the wrong job. Understanding preferred work styles and where a person would be happiest goes a long way to improving retention and productivity.

Pulling it All Together

The famous English scientist William Thomson, the Lord Kelvin, once said, "When you can measure what you are speaking about, and express it in numbers, you know something about it; but when you cannot measure it, when you cannot express it in numbers, your knowledge is of a meager and unsatisfactory kind. It may be the beginning of knowledge, but you have scarcely, in your thoughts, advanced to the stage of science, whatever the matter may be."

Science is the key to cracking the team building code. This is why when managers understand what really makes their people tick, they can create more productive teams. The key is using data to know the in-depth work style and personality traits of team members and to use that to motivate teams, communicate change, and delegate authority. Any business that wants to maximize productivity should be concerned with building a great team.

Once a person appreciates the why of team building, the logical next question is how. The how of cracking the team building code is the subject of the following chapter.

Team Building Code Crackers

Don't attempt to do team building on the cheap. Please *do not* use these tests for hiring teams.

DISC. The DISC system of assessing personality characteristics is based upon the work of psychologist William Marston, author of *The Emotions of Normal People.* After extensively studying the characteristics, patterns and responses of thousands of individuals, Marston developed an assessment in 1928 to measure four important behavioral factors. The factors he selected were Dominance, Influence, Steadiness and Cooperation, from which DISC takes its name. The DISC language of behavior has been validated in more than twenty-five countries since Marston introduced the model back in the Roaring '20s. This is not designed for candidate screening, only staff development.

Minnesota Multiphasic Personality Index. The MMPI was developed for mental patient profiling by Starke Hathaway. The Seventh Circuit Court of Appeals determined that the MMPI is a medical test. Per the guidelines of the Americans with Disabilities Act (ADA), it cannot, therefore, be used as a selection test prior to offering a candidate a job. In that sense, the MMPI is no different than a drug test or physical examination—still permissible, but not during the "pre-offer" stage.

Myers Briggs Type Indicator. The Myers-Briggs Type Indicator is exclusively intended for the purposes of career development and team building within a company, not as a hiring or promotion screen. Rather than tapping the Big Five personality characteristics, the Myers-Briggs test is based on the work of Carl Gustav Jung and addresses four areas of personality to create sixteen distinct types (the number sixteen is just a coincidence and not related to Cattell's work). The four areas are perception, judgment, extraversion and orientation toward the outside world. While the Myers-Briggs is used in many organizations and is very popular among employers and employees, there is little empirical evidence of its validity for employee selection.

Notes:

www.lighthouseconsulting.com

Chapter 2

Putting Your Teams to the Test

What criteria should you use to screen hiring tests and assessment companies? Naturally you want to know how long the profile has been around and what is the history. You should know how many people have used the test and in how many companies. Then you should dig deeper. Here is what we look for:

- Is the test properly validated and on what basis?

- Is the test reliable and on what basis?

- Is the test legal, and has it been reviewed for ADA compliance and gender, culture and racial bias?

- Would the test leave a negative impression with job candidates?

- Is it proper for both hiring and managing?

- Are enough scales used to cover the human personality?

- How much training or degrees are required to interpret the results?

- What reading level is required to take the test?

To help you screen in-depth work style and personality assessments (and testing companies), here is a nine-point checklist you can use to review assessment tools and support.

1.   Number of rating scales

The assessment company providing the test needs to disclose the number and type of ratings scales they are using. A rating scale is any instrument designed to assist in the measurement of subjective evaluations of, or reactions to, a person, object, event, statement, or other item of interest. The more rating scales, the clearer the picture.

According to the Encyclopedia of Psychology, several varieties of rating scales have been developed. One common form of rating scale presents the rater with a spectrum of potential responses that includes antithetical elements at each end of a range of intermediate possibilities, on which the rater is expected to indicate the position that most accurately represents the rater's response to the subject in question. Another form of rating scale presents the rater with a list of characteristics or attributes from which the rater is expected to select those which the rater believes apply to the subject in question. Rating scale instruments are used in psychological research primarily to assess qualities for which no objective answer ("Rating Scale." *Encyclopedia of Psychology*. 2nd ed. Ed. Bonnie R. Strickland. Gale Group, Inc., 2001. eNotes.com. 2006).

The number of scales does not determine the length of time it takes to take the profile. Some twelve scale profiles can take up to ninety minutes or more to complete, while the sixteen-scale profile can take thirty-five to forty-five minutes.

Using twelve or more scales is the most cost effective because the personality assessments can be used for both screening candidates and for team building. We feel this offers the best return on investment for a manager because they can first have their team test, and then use the data to best judge how new hires will work with the existing team.

2.   Amount of time it takes to take the test

How long should it take to complete a test? That depends on how in depth you need to look at personality. Here are your typical three options for testing:

- Basic team assessments using four primary scales with thirty to sixty questions can take ten to twenty minutes to complete.

- Simple prescreening of candidates/team assessments using up to eight scales with 60-120 questions can take twenty to thirty minutes to complete.

- In-depth personality tests for screening candidates and assessing the team using twelve to sixteen scales and more than 164 questions can take thirty-five to forty-five minutes to complete.

3.   Qualifications of the individual who is interpreting the test

In addition, we also believe the best tests require someone with comprehensive psychological training or degrees for proper interpretation of the data. Weekend training programs can be problematic since testing and human behavior is a very complex subject. When making hiring or internal decisions, organizations need as much information and understanding as possible as the consequences can be very costly.

4.   Link test to resume and job description

Data analysis of a potential new hire's personality is not enough. Before you hire this person, you will want to ascertain how the person's past relates to the possible future your position offers. Whoever is assessing the data of the candidate with the hiring manager needs to have the resume and the job description in order to do a thorough job of reviewing the data.

5.   Impression management/faking good scale

In our opinion, a questionnaire needs a minimum of 164 questions to gather enough data for an "impression management" scale. Impression management allows you to understand the accuracy of the results and if someone is trying to "fake good." A proper test analyzes personality characteristics in the context of business concerns:

- Coping with stress

- Interpersonal and social skills

- Problem solving

- Organizational role patterns

- Ability to get along with others

- Potential weaknesses

6. Thought flow

Of course, not everyone thinks and processes information the same way. A good in-depth and personality assessment will give you insight into an individual's thought flow. This not only helps with hiring, but understanding how someone's thoughts naturally flow is also a very powerful management tool. Sharing this information is just one more means of helping team members communicate more effectively with others.

7. Career matching

Certain personality tests help you gain information which may either support the person's present career choices or assist him or her to explore, consider and plan for another career direction. A personality test can give you an indication of which jobs match the candidate's personality type and which careers he or she may have an aptitude for. You do need to remember that the test results are only an indicator and should not be relied on as an absolute assessment of which career is best for the person.

8. Strengths and weaknesses summary

Using an in-depth work style and personality assessment is a proven and effective way to create highly functional teams. This starts with having a summary of each person's strengths and weaknesses. Once you know which personality types work best together, you can mix and match your people so that you get the most out of each of them. For every strength a person possesses, there is a corresponding weakness. Being assertive is a strength; however, that personality can be too assertive and off-putting for some people they deal with.

9. Detailed interview questions

The assessment company you choose should help you create tailored interview questions based on the job candidate's specific personality. The purpose is to develop interview questions that probe facets of the personality you need more details on. Many employers are now conducting behavioral interviews. Rather than focusing on resume and accomplishments alone, use an in-depth work style and personality assessment as a jumping off point to ask open-ended questions that will cause the job candidate to describe real circumstances and their responses to them. Ask them to describe in detail a particular event, project, or experience and how they dealt with the situation, and what the outcome was. This type of interviewing is the most accurate predictor of future performance.

www.lighthouseconsulting.com

Notes:

www.lighthouseconsulting.com

Part II

The How of Team Building

Chapter 3

Building Teams

When you think of a great team, what comes to your mind?

"For me, I'll never forget the day the underdog 1980 US Olympic ice hockey team won the gold medal," says Antarctic Mike Pierce.

Pierce, better known as Antarctic Mike, is a team-building expert who works with organizations that want to find, engage, and keep the best-performing people. He is the author of *The Penguin Principle: A Little Story About True Teamwork, Selling at 90 Below Zero,* and *Leading at 90 Below Zero.*

"The 1980 US Olympic ice hockey underdog win was not only one of the greatest sports moments ever, but it was one of the best examples of true team functioning at the highest level we'll ever see," says Pierce.

That is the type of team that any company would like to build.

"'On paper' they were not the most talented," adds Pierce. "They were not the fastest, strongest, or even a close favorite to medal, let alone win the gold. Against all odds, these underdogs accomplished what many teams dream of and few achieve."

For those truly interested in team building, this is a case study to consider. In the 2004 film *Miracle*, Kurt Russell stars as coach Herb Brooks in the true story of that 1980 US Olympic ice hockey team winning the gold medal by defeating the powerful Soviet Union and Finland teams at Lake Placid.

Brooks had a dream of coaching the US Olympic team ever since he was cut from the 1960 US Olympic team. His dream comes true, and he gets the coaching gig in 1979. He puts together a team of college kids and begins to get them into shape. Since the Soviet Union is the greatest hockey team in the world, Brooks begins to retrain his team in the European style of playing the game. These US college kids were true underdogs, because the "top dog" Soviet Union team had won four consecutive gold medals and had recently defeated a team of National Hockey League all-stars.

Brooks said that the problem with the NHL all-stars was that they were individual players and not a team. With all his hard training, he finally turns the Americans into a team and a family. In a Cinderella story, the US team defeats the Soviet Union in the semifinal round by not allowing them a single goal for the last ten minutes of the game, and then finished off powerful Finland in the final.

With the world watching the game on TV, sportscaster Al Michaels asks his famous question at the end of the game, "Do you believe in miracles? Yes!"

"There were many keys to that miracle on ice, but in the end it came down to one thing," says Pierce. "Each of the individuals cared more about their teammates than they did about themselves. They played their hearts out for the team, for the other players, for their coaches, and for their fans, but not for themselves. A team that plays at that level so selflessly is easy to admire, yet difficult to imitate in the world of business."

The True Greatest Team on Ice

However, there is a greater underdog team that takes to the ice and executes at high levels, Pierce tells us. Unlike the 1980 hockey Olympians, this is one team you probably would not picture if you were asked to think of a great team.

"This team is not a sports team, a business team or a professional association," says Pierce. "This team is not made up of people and very few of us have ever witnessed them in action. Yet they have as much to teach us about being a great team as any group that exists in the world."

In fact, to see this team in action, you have to travel very far. They are the emperor penguins who live in Antarctica, the true miracle on ice.

Pierce is an avid fan of polar expedition history and is an endurance athlete. In 2006, Mike became one of nine people to run the first-ever Antarctic Ice Marathon and a year later became the first American to run the Antarctic 100k, a grueling sixty-two miles on an ice shelf 600 miles from the South Pole. He was featured in *Sports Illustrated* and on ABC, CBS, CNN, ESPN, and Fox.

His flagship program, "Leading at 90 Below Zero," connects the drivers and principles of Antarctic expedition history stories to the real world of finding, engaging, and keeping great teams in today's business world.

"Perhaps you witnessed these magnificent creatures in the 2005 Academy Award-winning movie, *March of the Penguins*," says Pierce. "With narration by Morgan Freeman, the film is a look at the annual journey of emperor penguins as they march—single file—to their traditional breeding ground."

The film is a French nature documentary directed and co-written by Luc Jacquet, and co-produced by Bonne Pioche and the National Geographic Society. The film also tells an underdog story, a type of story that inspires many team builders.

Lessons from Antarctica on Building Teams

When building a team use in-depth work style and personality testing assessments to find team members who will apply what Pierce dubbed The Penguin Principle: True teamwork is putting the needs of others before your own.

The team goal for penguins is survival of the species. In autumn, all the penguins of breeding age (five years old and over) leave the ocean, their normal habitat, to walk inland to their ancestral breeding grounds. There, the penguins participate in a courtship that, if successful, results in the hatching of a chick. For the chick to survive, both parents must make multiple arduous journeys between the ocean and the breeding grounds over the ensuing months. It took one year for two isolated cinematographers to shoot the film.

"I travel throughout the US and Canada speaking to businesses, sales teams, professional associations and other groups on the subject of leadership and building stronger teams, using stories from Antarctic history to illustrate the points," says Pierce. "The most common question I get is, 'Why Antarctica?'"

Here's his short answer: Antarctica is much like the business world we live in. In Antarctica, you have conditions and circumstances that make survival and success very difficult, if not dangerous. Planning, preparing and executing with a well-conditioned team of people who function as one unit is imperative.

So, too, in the real world do businesses and teams of professional people face difficult, if not dangerous conditions every day. Think of the economy, the competition in your industry, the difficulties of communicating with and understanding people, and many other factors that are complicated. The degree that teams plan, prepare, condition themselves and function efficiently as a cohesive unit is the degree that they will be successful.

Consider how the emperor penguins in Antarctica accomplish this. What can business people learn from them about building strong teams that operate at high levels? These penguins are amazingly successful, despite the conditions being challenging.

How challenging? In Antarctica, the average daily year-round temperature is -58 degrees (F). It is the highest, driest, windiest, and coldest continent on earth. The emperor penguins are the only species who can survive such harshness. Year round they function as one team working together for a single purpose, to reproduce. Everything they do individually and collectively is aimed at this single task.

"There are many keys to their success," says Pierce. "For starters, consider their selflessness. Like the 1980 US Olympic Hockey team, the emperor penguins live their lives for each other, not for themselves. They spend almost all their waking time marching, but not alone. They cannot afford to fall behind or lose contact with their teammates or they will disappear into the whiteness of the Antarctic winter."

Their breeding ground is some seventy miles inland from the coast, and to march back and forth to accomplish their goal of successfully reproducing, they must march together. They must put the needs of the others ahead of themselves or survival won't happen. They will go for months without eating and display patience beyond belief. During the harshest part of the winter, they will huddle together in the rookery, taking turns at being on the outside of the huddle, where it is much colder and where they are far more exposed to the elements. Their only defense against the freezing cold is the group itself.

Emperor penguins do not operate hastily or move in a hurried fashion, but they are very consistent in their marching. No matter how cold, hungry or tired they are, they continue to march forward, knowing that their mate and offspring are depending on them.

Applying the Penguin Principle to Your Team Building

When you reflect on the emperor penguins, do you see the parallels to the real world? Teams today need to understand how to function together and depend on one another. This is not possible if the members are not willing and able to put the needs of others ahead of themselves. Ah, but how to find and train this kind of team member?

Of course, one of the advantages that today's business managers have is that they can choose who is on the team. Penguins don't have that luxury. Choosing the right "penguins for your team" is a critical first step. Making sure that the right people are in place for each particular role and keeping in mind how they'll function collectively, is one of the most important functions of a leader today. The question is how do you know how to select the right penguins for your team? "Unlike penguins, hiring is not black and white," says Pierce. "Traditional interviewing leaves you with some gray areas when it comes to candidates."

However, in-depth work style and personality assessments give hiring managers objective information to help make an informed decision about whether this person is a good fit for the job and for the team. If you decide to hire the person, the questions you ask during the hiring process will also reduce your learning curve as a manager on how best to manage this penguin from day one.

Team Building Code Crackers

Here are five ways to use in-depth work style and personality assessments to help bring out the best in your penguin employees:

1. Test the penguins first. Of course, candidates want to put their best foot forward during an interview. However, through a personality test and work style assessment, you uncover a great deal about their ability to work well with other personalities, their problem-solving abilities, their thought processes and their ability to tolerate stress.

2. Help your penguins be all that they can be. Everyone has strengths and weaknesses. Find out the real truth with an objective measure. Once you pinpoint the good and the bad, then you can place them in the right positions and coach them on where to improve.

3. Get all penguins to play nice. Sales and marketing, operations and financial people need to interact to make the company run smoothly. Too many employees get frustrated with other coworkers and wonder why everyone doesn't act like them. Managers can coach employees how to interact better with peers through the use of personality profiles and workplace assessments.

4. Treat coworker penguins the way they want to be treated. In today's fast-paced world of business there is little time to get to know many of your coworkers. Using personality assessments as the basis for team building exercises can quickly get everyone to have a healthier respect for other ways of seeing the world.

5. Forget tiger teams, pick better penguin teams. Today so much work is done by ad hoc "tiger teams" that come together for a specific purpose. Instead, you want "penguin teams" that accomplish miracles together. Before you assemble a team, it pays to know the strengths and weaknesses of the team members. Sometimes this can be the difference between a productive team that "wins the gold medal" and one that pulls apart at the seams.

Notes:

www.lighthouseconsulting.com

Chapter 4

Leading Teams

Before you assemble a team, it pays to know the strengths and weaknesses of the team members. When managers understand what makes their people tick, then they can be better leaders. Knowing in-depth work style and personality traits can help with motivating teams, communicating change and delegating authority.

Sometimes we hire the right employees and put them in the wrong jobs. Understanding preferred work styles and where a person would be happiest goes a long way to improving retention and productivity.

But how do you put that great data into action? When seeking to improve your ability to lead teams, consider these examples from some of the best teams around.

The Race to Build Better Teams

In the race to be a better leader of teams, are you open to a simple suggestion?

Leadership expert and author Boaz Rauchwerger recommends a quick team-building affirmation for leaders to say to themselves on a regular basis: "I ask for help when I need it."

As Speaker of the Year for Vistage International, the world's largest organization of CEOs, Rauchwerger has conducted hundreds of seminars for groups of CEOs throughout the U.S., Canada, Mexico, and the Caribbean. He has also spoken for such companies as American Airlines, Xerox, Toyota, and Jenny Craig.

For a lesson in what it means to lead teams, Rauchwerger suggests a visit to a city he recently spoke in: Charlotte, North Carolina. Just outside of the city is the Charlotte Motor Speedway, home of NASCAR races, many other events, and it's been the filming site for such movies as *Days of Thunder* and *Talladega Nights*.

Designed and built in 1959, this racetrack can now accommodate up to 171,000 spectators in its thousands of grandstand seats and luxury suites. It has the world's largest HDTV, measuring 200 feet wide and 80 feet tall. In 1984 it became the only sports facility in America to offer year-round living accommodations when forty condominiums were built high above turn one on the track.

"In addition to the excitement of cars traveling at up to 200 miles an hour, inches apart, on the 1.5 mile oval track, there is also a lot of excitement in pit row," observes Rauchwerger. "These days, NASCAR drivers need all the help they can get from their pit crews in order to win a race."

These support teams have turned into state-of-the-art choreographed examples of superb teamwork, notes Rauchwerger. "In twelve seconds or less, they can exchange four fresh tires and add eighteen gallons of gas. An extra second of efficiency can make the difference between winning and losing."

Rauchwerger, whose parents escaped from Europe in the late 1930s, was born in Israel. His family immigrated to the United States when he was nine. Although unable to speak the language at the time, he became a radio newscaster by the time he was in high school.

"In life, we all need help to win whatever race we're figuratively wanting to win," says Rauchwerger. "However, most people don't ask for help. In order for me to learn English when my family came to America, I needed the help of my high school speech teacher. I need the help of every audience member I'm in front of in order to deliver meaningful messages."

"People are honored when we ask them for help," says Rauchwerger. "I am honored when people ask me for help."

To be a better team leader, Rauchwerger suggests asking yourself a simple question:

"Who on my team could I ask for help with a problem or an important goal? Let's not delay. Every second could count."

Team Building the Army Way

Remember the old US Army slogan: "In the Army, we do more before 9 a.m. than most people do all day"?

Non-army personnel may be tempted to believe that productivity comes from command-and-control leadership exercised daily by those with the highest rank, with little regard given to team building.

But contrary to what many believe, the Army is about teamwork.

"For many folks not in the military there is a common misperception that the Army operates in a strict hierarchical-structured environment," says Brigadier General Jeffrey Foley, US Army retired.

"There is some truth to that, especially during times of crisis when quick decisions need to be made," concedes Foley. "However, the vast majority of time, when life is not on the line, nothing could be further from the truth."

Today Foley is an author, speaker, and leadership development facilitator. He is the coauthor of the book *Rules & Tools for Leaders* and author of *Building Winning Cultures.*

"To volunteer to willingly give up one's life as a soldier for a greater cause is perhaps the most profound example of leadership," says Foley. "Soldiers join the military for a host of reasons. One major reason why soldiers choose to stay is the experience they shared becoming a band of brothers and sisters, that special fraternity called the profession of arms."

The team leaders of the enlisted branch of the army are called sergeants. The origin of the term sergeant is from the Latin serviens, which means "one who serves." So, at the very core of the army, the focus is on sergeants as those who serve.

"In 1978, I landed at Fort Bragg, North Carolina on my initial assignment out of West Point," recall Foley. "Fort Bragg was the home of the Airborne. On the day of my arrival, I was met by the senior enlisted soldier of the battalion, Command Sergeant Major Tad Gaweda, a tough, battle-hardened veteran soldier and marvelous leader. He taught me that first day, 'Every soldier has a sergeant. Don't ever forget that.' His message was clear to me: listen to your sergeant for he will teach you well."

Foley contends one of the most profound leadership skills in any military organization is the ability to listen. His mentor, Perry Smith (Major General, US Air Force, Retired), calls it "squinting with your ears."

The Army does not have professional privates or lieutenants. It is either up or out: soldiers get promoted or leave. Those who demonstrate leadership potential earn the opportunity to continue to serve.

"When it comes to soldiering, what is the biggest differentiator between the army of the United States and all other countries?" asks Foley. "Simply put, the difference is the monumental investment in the training and leadership development of our professional non-commissioned officer (NCO) corps— our sergeants. We call our NCOs the backbone of our army because we rely on them so heavily."

How the Army Trains Teams

Foley is fond of quoting the words of General Creighton Abrams, former US Army chief of staff: "Soldiers are not in the army. Soldiers are the army."

The Army develops soldiers in three ways.

"First, millions of dollars are invested in the professional soldiers through periodic formal assessments, training, and education. Second, every Army unit is required to have an organic leader development program to help develop leaders. Third, on the job coaching and mentoring by every non-commissioned officer and officer to help grow subordinate leaders. In the army, succession planning is everyone's job, every day."

In the business world these actions are referred to as succession planning.

While there is clear rank structure in the army, true leadership comes to life when mutual trust between leaders and followers exists. Trust is earned by leaders who live the values, are competent in their technical and tactical skills, and genuinely care about their people.

"When there is a lack of trust in a military unit, the consequences are significant: decisions are questioned, commitment evaporates, discipline erodes, and the unit becomes ineffective," says Foley. "It does not take long to create an environment of distrust."

And when team building works in the US Army, what is the result?

"In the best units I served, I felt the love and support of those around me," says Foley. "I knew they would come to my aid if needed. I did my best to stay confident in my own abilities, and let go of my ego. I did that because the best leaders I observed did the same."

Team Building Code Crackers

1. Know the strengths and weaknesses of the team members. Understanding preferred work styles and where a person would be happiest goes a long way to improving retention and productivity.

2. Many leaders are afraid to groom a high-performing employee for promotion, because they hate to lose someone good. Wrong, wrong, wrong. Your job as a manager is to help people grow, and then find the right new employees to replace them.

3. Team building is something that should be done on a regular, continual basis. If you do it episodically, then the employees tend to look at it as something the leaders do when something is wrong or when you get a big order. Communicating on a monthly or quarterly basis is something to strive for, but not less than every six months.

4. Don't neglect the social side. Functions like the company picnic and the holiday party are important. So is the celebration for the big win. In our experience, companies who celebrate victories do better over time.

5. Breaking bread is also a proven strategy. Regularly take a cross section of employees out for a lunch discussion. If you show genuine interest in your employees, they will know that you care. Then they are more likely to open up to you on what is really going on. Tagalongs are another strategy. Have a less-experienced employee shadow you for some client meetings, lunches and project work.

6. Overall, the leading team's payoff can be enormous. Never forget it is the leader's job to create employee alignment with personal goals, management objectives, and company goals. Using information gleaned from assessment will help build better players and deeper bench strength.

Notes:

www.lighthouseconsulting.com

Chapter 5

Motivating Teams

In today's fast-paced world of business there is little time to get to know many of your team members. Using in-depth work style and personality assessments as the basis for team motivation can quickly get everyone to have a healthier respect for other ways of seeing the world.

A main message of this book is that the days of seat-of-the-pants motivation are over. There is too much science to ignore. When managers understand what makes their people tick, then they can be better team motivators. Knowing the work style and personality traits of your employees can help with motivating teams, communicating change and delegating authority.

Team motivation often takes place during team meetings, which can be a challenge for many organizations. Typical team meetings are demotivational, but that doesn't have to be the case.

Make Team Meetings Motivating

Let's face facts: employees commonly feel that team meetings are a waste of time; however, it doesn't have to be that way if the meeting leader takes the time to make meetings meaningful, productive, and even fun.

"We need to bring business meetings into the digital age in the same way that we have reinvented business planning and written communication," says former Harvard Business School professor Jim Ware, Ph.D., author of the book *Making Meetings Matter: How Smart Leaders Orchestrate Powerful Conversations in the Digital Age*.

Ware has invested his entire career in understanding what organizations must do to thrive in a rapidly changing world. His business wisdom comes from deep academic knowledge and over thirty years of hands-on experience as a senior executive and a change leader driving corporate innovation.

Ware says leaders should think of a team meeting as an improv performance; the most important mindset you can establish is to have a basic plan but then be in the moment, reacting both instinctively and creatively to events as they evolve in real time.

"The most significant thing you can do as a meeting leader to ensure that any particular conversation is meaningful is to approach it with a positive, growth-oriented mindset," says Ware. "If there is one skill that matters most to leading meetings that matter, it is the ability to think and respond quickly as a conversation unfolds."

Presumably you defined the meeting agenda and told the other participants how you want the conversation to unfold. "If you ignore that agenda, or go off topic, you are implicitly giving everyone else permission to do the same thing," warns Ware. "That makes it much more difficult to rope someone else in when they've gone off on a tangent."

Motivational Magic at the Intersection of Personality and Purpose

To ensure an organization's long-term success, pursuing purposeful behavior is the best motivational practice business leaders can follow for thriving in today's stakeholder-driven world. Employee teams are, of course, a key stakeholder.

"Purposeful behavior means taking actions that are consistent with a purpose that is meaningful and important to all the organization's stakeholders," says Paul Ratoff, author of the book *Thriving in a Stakeholder World: Purpose as the New Competitive Advantage*.

Ratoff has been a successful business consultant in Southern California for the past thirty-five years, assisting a wide range of middle-market companies plan and manage their growth and success. He is a Certified Management Consultant and president of Strategy Development Group.

His book demonstrates to business leaders that purpose can be the driving force behind a better management style and can also provide a competitive advantage in their markets.

Here are five practices Ratoff recommends to business leaders seeking to motivate their teams through a shared meaningful purpose for their company:

1. Ask Why? Challenge yourself by continually asking the simple question, "Why is this meaningful and important to me?" until you are inspired. Start with the reason you wanted to go into business in the first place and then ask the "why" question. Keep asking that question until you come to an answer which you find inspiring or moving in some way. Look for a problem your business solved for people.

2. Ask What Really Inspires You. You can also look for actions you would like to take on in your life that inspire you. Something you are doing or might want to do outside of business, if only you had the time or money. Maybe there is a hobby you would love to take on, or a charity you are supporting, or a cause that is important to you. Then, consider how your business might serve as a vehicle to pursue that interest.

3. Think Beyond Business Model. Do not limit yourself to the things your organization does to make money. Purpose and business model are very different. Think of your products and services as byproducts of your organization's purpose. For example, a company could be committed to creating leaders in the world but it trains and develops its leaders inside of a vertical retail-store/e-commerce business model.

4. Expand on Your Product's Value. By the same token, the product or service could also be the source of your passion. If that is true, you can use the "why" question to better understand the passion behind it. The value you bring to your customers can be defined as having three levels: There is the physical level of the product or service that is often defined by its specifications and characteristics. There is also the emotional level that is defined by how it affects one personally—for example, how it feels or tastes or comforts. Then there is the conceptual level, which has more to do with how it will impact the world—for example, reduce crime, improve overall health, reduce hunger, etc.

5. Look at Personal Goals. By personal goals, Ratoff is referring to goals that affect you directly, such as buying a house, becoming a thought leader, etc. Personal goals are very different than purpose. If you consider the time horizon, personal goals are generally achieved in a much shorter time period, say from one to five years. They only need to be inspiring to one person: you. Purpose, on the other hand, would need to have a much longer time horizon, which could extend beyond many generations.

"Purpose needs to be inspiring to many more people, specifically, the organization's key stakeholders," says Ratoff. "It is not uncommon for leaders to mistake personal goals as their organization's purpose. For example, being the largest company in the industry may be a personal goal but it would not likely be an organization's purpose. It might be a shorter-term goal if it supported the organization's purpose and business strategy."

Team Building Code Crackers

The following are Jim Ware's top ten ways a leader can make meetings more motivating for teams:

1. Assume that the team is far more intelligent and experienced than any single participant. Remember, no one is smarter individually than everyone together. And that includes you.

2. Presume that team members can learn and grow. And that also includes you. Be open to learning from anyone about anything. Remember that you are already in a position of leadership; you don't have to prove that you are smarter or better informed than the other participants

3. Focus on broad goals that everyone agrees with. Start the conversation with common goals and seek win/win solutions whenever possible.

4. Respect individual differences. Remember that there is only one of you, and there is only one of everybody else in the world. There is almost infinite synergy available when you focus on drawing out those individual differences to leverage the diverse strengths within the group.

5. Be mindful of other team member responsibilities, constraints, and needs. Unless you believe it is unavoidable, don't ask the meeting participants to make commitments or agree with positions that will make their own lives more difficult. Respecting their individual circumstances

---

includes avoiding putting them into difficult positions or endangering their personal and professional relationships.

6. Suspend judgment. Hear out team members and be sure you understand their ideas in sufficient depth before you decide (and certainly before you communicate) whether those ideas are useful and relevant, or a distraction.

7. Enter every conversation with an open and curious mind. You just never know what experiences and relevant knowledge the other participant(s) might bring to the conversation.

8. Look for common ground. Find areas of agreement, or at least where the participants' insights overlap. Build on that sense of commonality to move toward consensus, or at least to find something that everyone can agree on.

9. Be authentic. Admit it when you don't know an answer, or when you need help. Express the emotions you are experiencing; for example, if someone comes up with an exciting and innovative idea, thank them or praise them (but only if you genuinely mean it).

10. Reinforce constructive behaviors from others. When someone else offers thanks, or praise, thank them in turn. Reward behaviors that help move the conversation forward, and over time you will see more of them.

Notes:

www.lighthouseconsulting.com

Chapter 6

Compensating Teams

Typically Beth Carroll is asked, "What is the right way to pay my team?"

"But there is no easy answer to this question," says Carroll, founder of Prosperio Group and author of the book *Taming the Compensation Beast.*

"The right way to compensate teams depends on a variety of factors particular to each company;" says Carroll. However, there are some definite *wrong ways* to pay (for a more detailed discussion we recommend her excellent book that came out in 2017).

This chapter highlights Carroll's six most common mistakes for compensating a team. The information is based on her work as compensation consultant with hundreds of private and public companies from a variety of industries, ranging in size from small privately held companies to multi-billion-dollar global giants.

Mistake #1: Not realizing that compensation is part of a complex and interconnected system.

There are two variations to this mistake. In the first, managers fail to understand that compensation both supports and reflects a company's unique objectives, strategy, structure, and culture. When leaders want us to just "tell them the answer," or "tell them how XYZ company pays," or when they think they can just use the plan from their last company, they are making this mistake.

In order to develop the right plan for your company, there is no easy answer—you are going to have to do some work.

The second variation to this mistake is to develop compensation plans for highly interconnected roles separately from one another. We are often asked for a plan for sales, or for operations, or for account managers, because that may be a particular pain point at that moment. However, it is likely that a change to the incentive plan for any one of these roles will have a ripple effect on the other roles. It's not easy, but the right way to develop new incentive plans is to consider <u>all</u> of the roles in your organization at once so you can be sure the plans encourage people to work together and not against each other.

Mistake #2: Thinking about compensation as only an economic deal with the employees.

Compensation is about more than money and those who think about only the math are missing at least half of the point. We tell our clients that using an incentive plan is like putting a megaphone on your business strategy. Whatever is in the incentive plan will get a disproportionate amount of attention from employees, so isn't it sensible to spend time thinking about the message being sent? The plan shouts to employees the company's priorities, ethics, team philosophy, how valuable they are (or aren't) to management, and how much opportunity they have for growth and advancement. Getting the psychology of incentives right is at least as important as getting the math right.

Another mistake in this category is to think about incentive compensation only from the perspective of "how much can I afford to pay." In the sales compensation world this is called a "cost of sales" philosophy. As organizations mature and cash flow becomes less of a concern, management recognizes that knowing the market value of a job is important to attract and retain the type of talent they want. This is called a "cost of labor" philosophy and is used by all sophisticated companies once they reach a certain maturity and size. It is at this point that compensation surveys become very important and companies look to the market to understand what is required to pay a competitive wage (and what isn't).

Another economic mistake is to think that if a little incentive is a good thing, then a lot of incentive must be better. It is rare that paying 100 percent variable pay to employees (100 percent commission plan) is a good thing. Employers lose almost all control when an employee has no salary. The employees may engage in practices that are detrimental to the company's business, customers, carriers, and ethics. The employees are also more likely to jump ship with "their" customers… (excuse me, *whose* customers?)

and go for a better offer or start up their own company based on the training, marketing, and technological support *you* gave them.

While a bit of hunger can be a good thing to drive performance, desperation is rarely an effective motivational tool for the long term. If you want your employees to act like used car sales people, or to run your business the way subprime mortgage brokers ran theirs, then by all means use a 100 percent variable approach. (Tip: AIG and Lehman Brothers were big success stories once upon a time and everyone wanted to know their secrets. One of those secrets was a highly variable and highly leveraged incentive plan, which rewarded excessive risk taking and was a proximate cause of the economic collapse of 2008).

Mistake #3: Not considering short-term and long-term unintended consequences.

Short-term consequences from ill-designed incentive plans typically involve damaging customer relationships and damaging employee interactions. For example, if a plan puts too much pressure on profit, you might find your employees negotiating too hard with your customers and costing the company current business, and worse--the opportunity for future business. Likewise, if a plan rewards only individual performance, then employees may work against each other to maximize their own paychecks.

Long-term consequences are harder to anticipate because, by definition, the effects do not manifest themselves for months or even years. The most common long-term consequence is sacrificing long-term growth for short-term gain. This is often found among group managers whose incentive plans pay a percentage of profit. Group managers may resist hiring employees under this type of plan as they will inevitably take a short-term hit in their incentive compensation while they train the new employee. Everyone will agree that in the long run the group will increase in performance, but managers rarely have the kind of long-term vision as entrepreneurial owners; they are worried about their mortgage and the next car payment. Owners or senior leaders, by definition, are more willing to take risks than employees, and they are more likely to see the long-term benefit from making "investment" decisions. *Hint: If your employees were willing to take these kinds of risks they wouldn't be working for you.*

Mistake #4: Not clarifying goals to enable the shift from transactional to growth-focused plans.

The most common complaint from business owners is the inability to grow. You need to make your growth goals clear, to yourself and your employees, or there is no accountability when you fail to reach them or celebrations when you do. You also need to pay using performance expectations, as this will drive employees to higher levels of performance. At a minimum, you need to use three levels: Threshold, Target, and Excellence.

Threshold is the minimum level of performance required to earn an incentive. If your employees have a base salary, there should be minimum level of performance before incentives kick-in. However, it's rarely a good idea to make this an explicit function of their salary (though I'm well-aware many organizations do this). Effective compensation design actually separates salary and incentives into two different categories of compensation. Salary increases should be earned for teamwork, punctuality, attitude and any number of other intangibles that differentiate a good employee from a problematic one. Incentives should be used to reward performance in areas that are objective, measurable, relevant to the business, and controllable by the employee. Many brokers miss this opportunity to reward (or correct) the intangibles by never giving salary increases, tying salary increases only to productivity, or tying incentive thresholds to salary (which actually makes any salary increase feel like a punishment).

As a good rule of thumb, 90 percent of your employees should be at or above threshold in any pay period, and payout at threshold should be anywhere between 1 percent and 25 percent of the target incentive. If this figure is not being achieved, your incentive plan is not providing much in terms of motivational value.

Target is the level of performance expected from an average performer and should bear some relationship to the growth goals of the organization (the sum of the targets for all employees should equal or slightly exceed the overall company goal). We often refer to a concept called "Target Incentive Compensation." This is the amount of incentive pay earned when target performance is attained. When added to the salary, this becomes Target Total Compensation. When you look at what an employee actually earned in a year (salary plus all cash incentive payments), this is called Actual Total Compensation and is the only number that could be compared across companies. Some companies pay more in salary and less in incentive than others. Some companies use a pure commission approach, others use a commission combined with team incentives, bounties, or other payout mechanics. Comparing just the base salary misses anything from incentives. Likewise, comparing just the commission rate does not factor in the salary or if any pay is coming from other components, such as a quarterly team payout. Be wary of companies who report inflated Target Total Compensation. A true Target Total Compensation figure should be achievable by 50-60 percent of the population. If a company is telling prospective employees (or competitors) that their Target Total Compensation is a figure that has only been achieved by one employee in the last five years, they are deceiving themselves, prospects, and the market at large.

Mistake #5: Not understanding the legal ramifications of incentive compensation.

Most of you are (or should be) aware that the misclassification of an employee as exempt from overtime pay can have significant legal and financial ramifications for your company, but you may not be aware that there are also rules that govern incentive compensation as well. For starters, you should be aware that if an employee is non-exempt (paid overtime) and they are on an incentive plan then their incentive pay needs to be factored into the rate used to calculate their overtime pay. Your payroll company should be doing this for you automatically, as this is common knowledge. Of course, for exempt employees who are not paid overtime, this is a non-issue.

Many states also have rules about the handling of certain calculations which are common in commission plans and you should check with local legal counsel that specialize in labor laws in any state in which your employees work. Of particular concern are "holdbacks" or "chargebacks." Some states frown on the notion that an employee can have earned an incentive, but the company is holding that pay pending the performance of some future event (such as payment by a customer). It is far better to simply say that the incentive has not been earned until that event actually happens. Chargebacks can also be problematic as you are now taking money away that was already paid. Likewise, there are states that have rules about how and when employees (or agents) may be entitled to pay after they separate from the company. If you think that you are not liable for payments after an employee leaves the company, you may find out the hard way that is not the case if your plan documents have not been worded carefully and signed by the employee to make it clear what happens after termination.

While the world at large tends to use the word *commission* to mean *any variable pay paid to a sales rep*, and *bonus* to mean a *discretionary year-end payout*, compensation consultants use the word *commission* to mean a mathematical formula that determines payout as a percentage of revenue or profit. A *bonus,* or a goal-based incentive, is *a formula that determines payout based on actual results in relation to a defined goal.* Under a commission plan, someone who sells more makes more. Under a goal-based bonus plan, the person who exceeds his/her goal by the greatest percentage will make the most. For whatever reason, state labor laws scrutinize the structure and rules of goal-based bonus plans less than they do commission plans. Therefore, we recommend using the word *commission* only when it means exactly what state legislatures interpret it to mean (a percent of revenue of profit) and using the term *incentive compensation* when talking about variable pay of any sort. This just helps keep things from getting messy…why would you want to be scrutinized on your *commission* plan when it's not really even technically a commission?

Mistake #6: Not communicating and supporting the plans, and not following up with solid tracking and feedback.

If you've managed to avoid all the other mistakes, but you still make this one then you will be no better off than when you started. In fact, you may be worse off because now you will have lost credibility with your staff. When you launch a new incentive plan, you need to back it up. You need to explain it, explain it again, and then explain it again. People have numerous preconceived ideas about incentive compensation based on what they have seen in the past and they will see any new incentive plan through this lens. It can be very difficult to change this mindset and you may not realize the points of miscommunication until after you've made the first or second payout under the new plan. It takes two to three pay cycles for employees to truly internalize a new compensation plan. It's only at this point that you will really start to see lasting change in behavior. If you have not reinforced the plan, shown them performance results and discussed how they can improve the next time, then you will not get the gains that you need from your plan.

The communication approach to incentive compensation should be as methodical as the design approach. First, you need to be sure your leadership team is on-board with the new design and will support the change. This includes managers and team leaders who will likely be the first line of defense for dealing with complaints (and there *will be* complaints.). Bring them into the process early to get their input and buy-in. Then, consider a phased approach for communication.

Even now you are not done. You need to provide regular performance reports so employees can monitor their results ahead of their payouts. You will gain nothing if they only find out on the day they get their check if they did a good job or a bad job. They should know ahead of time so they can adjust.

Final Thoughts on Compensating the Team

"The best managers provide constant coaching and feedback and the incentive plan is a perfect excuse to do this." Says Carroll. "You want them to make as much money as possible, don't you?" You should, if your plan is designed well because then the company is also making a lot of money. Your interests should be directly aligned with their interests.

By coaching the team and communicating with them about their incentives, you will be working together to maximize their results. They will be happy and your company will see motivated employees driving profitable growth for the company.

Team Building Code Crackers

When you write your team compensation plan documents, put some thought into how exceptions will be handled. You will not be able to think of everything, but some common points of contention are:

- Vacations or days off: will employees cover for each other? Will you guarantee a payout?
- New hires: is there a probationary period or a guaranteed payout during the first few months?
- Terminations: when is the last payment on the incentive plan?
- Transfers: how would you pro-rate between plans?
- Splitting credit *(hint: avoid it if at all possible)*
- Disciplinary action: if someone is under a performance warning, will they get an incentive?
- Gaming the system *(our advice…do not tolerate this at all, terminate immediately)*

Notes:

www.lighthouseconsulting.com

Part III

Sustaining the Team

Chapter 7

Managing Difficult Teams

As a manager, you must deal with a wide range of personalities on your team. Thanks to proper hiring assessments, most of your team members should be productive and reasonable workers.

Ah, but difficult team members are a way of life. Maybe you inherited them. Or they slipped through the hiring screens. Perhaps they came your way in a restructuring move.

Regardless, difficult team members are an obstacle to high performance. The objective is to handle the difficulty without difficulty.

Difficult Team Members Are Annoying

"Why listen to me?" asks Ilene Marcus. "I can be difficult. It's true. I talk too fast, think too fast, and get to the heart of the matter quickly, probably before you want to get there. That also makes me annoying."

Marcus, author of the book *Managing Annoying People*, was a key player in Mayor Rudy Giuliani's administration in New York City.

"My management career went from zero to sixty mph in the blink of an eye," says Marcus. "Starting as a social worker advocating for change when Mayor Giuliani took office in 1994, he made me an offer I couldn't refuse. Welfare reform was one of his top three priorities in his first term. I was suddenly dropped into the deep end of the pool to manage a notoriously difficult bureaucracy with 10,000 staff for a welfare system of 1.2 million clients that was spiraling out of control. Yes, the really deep end of the pool."

Marcus discovered there are no blanket solutions for dealing with difficult team members. Each situation needs to be tackled individually. The road to take is not to address what annoys you, but instead to follow the path about your reaction to the annoyance. How you handle the difficult team members and keep the behavior from sabotaging the team is the test of a great leader.

"Management styles may differ and work places evolve, but human nature remains constant," advises Marcus. "It is inevitable that someone on your team will be difficult. Like the Boy Scouts, be prepared. It's a good motto."

In general, says Marcus, and all else being equal (no mental illness, life crisis, or other intangibles) managers who are annoyed with difficult team members respond with four basic reactions:

Fight—right back at them, flinging the dirt, showing who is boss and being difficult yourself

Flight—turn and run, avoid at all costs, don't engage

Freeze—stuck, not sure what to do or what to say, so I will ignore the annoyance

Focus—gather your basket of tactics and manage full speed ahead

Often, reactions to difficult team members are complicated and can overlap each other. How your team sees you react is more important than the difficult behavior that is disrupting the team.

"Your goal is to focus," says Marcus. "Use your prowess and combine it with expertise to get out of the trap. You must set the tone as the team leader and minimize the office drama and impact on productivity. To do this, you need to have difficult team members marching in tune with the rest of the band. And you need to be leading the team to a harmonious existence."

Marcus offers these tips for dealing with difficult team members:

Look at this through the forest lens. Individual trees make up the forest, but the forest is much more than each tree. It's an ecosystem with changes in one species impacting the entire woodland. This is not just about your relationship with one direct report. This relationship is magnified by how the team sees you react to this person. It's fed with how they see you treat this person. It sets the stage for how they interpret your actions and then in turn decide how they should treat this person, each other and ultimately, you as the leader. Your action must be subtle enough to turn the situation in a new direction, yet strong enough to make an impact on the entire team.

Model how you would like difficult team members who are annoying you to be treated. In meetings where the whole team is present, patterns are set and seen by all. You cannot assume that your team is behind you based on the facts. Your behavior is a variable you must take into account.

Quantify, strategize, and recover. The key to understanding the impact on productivity is quantifying the hours spent processing why you are annoyed, strategizing how to get less annoyed, and then recovering from being annoyed. To harness new found time, energy and rapport with your staff, you must fully appreciate what the annoying trap is currently costing you and the company. The payoff to overcoming the wasted time is the new-found creativity, insight, and clarity of purpose. When you link your energy drain to the rest of the team, you will be driven to master the skills of managing difficult behaviors that impede productivity.

Think culture. Your company's culture is embodied in the core mission, values, beliefs and style of the founder and the management team. The culture is the intangible glue that holds all the pieces of the company together in a cohesive package. It's the special sauce in a good company that makes the sum greater than all the individual parts. It's executed through your policy, practices and interactions between employees, customers and business partners. It's felt by your employees through compensation decisions, talent sourcing, investment in professional development and emphasis on quality and ethics.

"As a boss, there is an economic contract between the team and the manager," says Marcus. As manager, your job is to provide the tools, resources, direction and rules to meet their work obligations. Being inspirational, motivational and wise, are righteous perks, once the minimum requirements are met. "All good management relationships are built on the foundation of clear role definition, expectations, and results. That's the basis of the work relationship between a manager and team members, including a CEO and his direct reports."

How to Course Correct

Know any Jennifers? Alan Cohen, author of *The Connection Challenge*, says every business has difficult team members, workers who are uncivil, mean-spirited, rude, dismissive, selfish, and combative. Cohen shares the following example of how coaching based on assessment feedback made a difference for Jennifer:

> *Jennifer was a forty-year-old PR account director on the fast track. A type-A personality, she was driven for success. But Jennifer was not winning much favor from her employees. They found that her feedback was often given in a drive-by manner and left them feeling like they were run over. She was all about results, and didn't ever take time to notice how her abrasive manner was impacting morale. She rarely gave praise and was overly critical of everyone's performance. To turn the situation around, her company provided her coaching, including 360° feedback from her team. While she was glad her bosses thought that she was a high achiever, she was crushed to learn that her employees felt that she was insensitive. She actually did care about her team, and assumed they knew that. After she recovered from the ego bruising, she took more time to notice how others were responding to her. She worked on being more patient. She realized that the extra few minutes she took to give feedback, to offer praise, to listen and to demonstrate empathy actually improved her team's performance. Her results were beyond expectations. Jennifer was soon promoted, and her team felt supported and appreciated.*

In his book, Cohen offers these eight common difficult-team-member scenarios and how to improve the situation.

1. Judgment and cynicism. Have you ever been in a conversation with someone and suddenly felt like they were silently judging you? (Notice the eyeroll, the tone of voice, the lecture.) Or have you tried to connect with someone who constantly hides behind a wall of cynical commentary and perspective on the world? These behaviors act as barriers to connection and can break the trust needed for healthy relationships. If you notice judgment and/or cynicism coming up in a connection—whether from your end or the other person—take a moment to stop, slow down, and see how you can come back to a place of connected authenticity. Check in with the other person to see how they're *really* doing. How can you bring more honesty and love into the connection? Often, the judgment and cynicism is masking some fear or anxiety underneath. Use empathy to keep it real. As human beings, our ability to perceive and evaluate is a gift. Know when you are using your critical thinking skills and abilities to reason versus projecting "my way is the better or only way."

2. Hotheads and bullies. To paraphrase the Billy Joel song, while there might be a place in the world for the Angry Young Man, too much ranting can tear down relationships. People may find themselves on edge around a person with a quick trigger or who puts down others. They may not want to share important information or voice a contrary opinion. If you find yourself raging or bullying, notice what triggers you and create a strategy for releasing that anger (breathe, take a break, get some exercise, see a therapist). If you are on the receiving end, speak up and ask for your colleague to dial it down, or empathize so they know they are being heard. That often will diffuse the situation.

3. Lack of appreciation or acknowledgement. A fast way to build connection is to express a genuine appreciation or acknowledgement for the other person. So naturally, the reverse of this is an instant connection killer. It takes about a minute to give authentic praise or acknowledgement, not much time at all — but it can mean the world to the person on the receiving end.

4. Knowing it all. We all like to share what we know, and to express our knowledge to those around us. However, it is vital to maintain an awareness of the other person, and what they share. Keeping a certain level of humility and interest in the other person's ideas and contributions is key to keeping a connection strong. Connection is always far more important than taking credit for being right. In our multi-generational workplace, those with more gray hair may sometimes dismiss the knowledge and insights of those younger. When they do, they miss a significant opportunity to learn and stay relevant. When those younger ones profess to know it all, they miss out on opportunities to learn from those who may have more life experience, and breadth of knowledge.

5. Lack of curiosity. A closed mind, closed heart, and lack of curiosity are instant connection shut-downs. Without curiosity, this person is essentially conveying that their beliefs are set, and they will gain nothing by interacting with you. Time to walk away from *that* connection, right? A healthy dose of curiosity and an almost childlike wonderment of the world will draw people to you, as you emit an open vibe that's delightful to connect with. Your curiosity will rub off on others, enhancing their experience of life as well!

6. Compare and despair. We may find ourselves comparing ourselves to the other person with whom we are interacting and concluding that we don't measure up. In that moment, we are forgetting things that make us awesome. Social media can also fuel low self-esteem. We see only a small part of our friends' and colleagues' lives, generally more the highs than the lows. When we compare, we despair. We lose touch with those things we have in common. We forget our own awesomeness.

7. Emotionally tone deaf. The colleague who fails to recognize that what he is saying is hurtful or insensitive, the boss who is clueless that the request that she is making of you the first day you are back from a family funeral is unreasonable—a lack of emotional awareness of the feelings of others diminishes trust and creates walls. These behaviors, over time, can tear down relationships, diminish trust, and have employees packing up their desks and clients taking their business to your competitor. Acknowledging and validating the feelings of others goes miles to create business harmony. Golden Rule: let people know you care, and that they are seen and heard.

8. No boundaries. One must always be aware of political and cultural sensitivities—you never know what another person values, what his or her culture embraces, and where someone stands on the important issues. Particularly in a business environment, off-color jokes, political diatribes, stories of sexual conquests or weekend binge drinking is risky discourse. While being authentic goes far to build relationships, balancing our need to speak our mind or share our personal exploits with good sense and good manners is generally a good idea.

A failure to see anything other than black or white can project an image of small mindedness and narrow perspective and leaves little room for discussion and understanding. If you think you may be coming across as believing there is only one approach, course correct. Become more open to new possibilities. If you notice someone else is projecting this way of thinking, gently offer some other ways of seeing the situation.

Team Building Code Crackers

During our workshops on managing difficult people, we always express a debt of gratitude to Rick Brinkman and Rick Kirschner, authors of the books *Dealing With People You Can't Stand* and *Dealing with Difficult People* (for a detailed review of their work, please see chapter 8 on "How to Manage Difficult People" in our 2008 book *Cracking the Personality Code*, which used information from the two doctors with their permission). Here is a quick list of the five types of difficult team members Brinkman and Kirschner say you will have to deal with on the road to high performance:

The Authority: "I know it all." Use them as resources by letting them know you recognize them as experts.

The Fake: "Look at me." Give them a little attention by repeating back their comments with enthusiasm.

The No Person. "No! No! No!" Allow them to be negative. Don't fight with them.

The Whiner. "Oh, woe is me!" Don't try to solve their problems, because you can't.

The Yes Person. "I just can't say no!" Make it safe to talk about fear and anger, and expect to deal with broken promises.

Notes:

www.lighthouseconsulting.com

Chapter 8

Keeping Teams on Track

Ken Ude is a man who knows a thing or two about keeping a team on track. Literally on track. Ude is the CEO of the Jim Russell Racing Drivers School at Sears Point in Sonoma, California.

"Find a successful company and you'll find a management team that is functioning like a fine-tuned race engine," says Ude.

Here are some things Ude has found successful over the years that have helped to keep teams on track:

Conduct an annual planning meeting. Go through a formal planning process with your front-line team to assess your competitive position and set your priorities for the year. Develop both strategic and tactical initiatives. Get to know how your people are "wired" and how they might function as a team by using professional help. Do this in advance. It can really help if things get tough in the future. Get buy-in on the total planning process. Assign responsibilities and identify milestones. And yes, make sure the milestones are measurable and achievable. *If it can be measured ~ it can be improved.*

Have regular review meetings. At least monthly review the financial performance of the company with your team and review the progress you are making on your plan.

Create a loose and casual atmosphere. Ude believes a relaxed atmosphere encourages front-line team members to provide open and honest feedback. Without it, you are lost.

Focus on the Ps. On a weekly basis review the status and progress of your **P**eople, **P**rograms, **P**riorities and make sure your watch your **P**ennies.

Get away from the office. The annual planning meeting, customer rewards and employee appreciation events are best done away from the office in an environment where everyone can participate on an equal basis and at a location where you can combine business with pleasure.

"I have been involved in a number of different companies and have participated in scores of different team-building events from golf to fishing," says Ude. "In all my years I have never seen a more unique and memorable event as a racing or performance driving experience at Sears Point Raceway in Sonoma. For some reason people love to compete in high-adrenaline team-building driving adventure. Perhaps because it is really unique and not something that most people get a chance to do."

If you are looking for a unique getaway for your team, consider a Racing or Driving Adventure at the Jim Russell Racing Drivers School at Sears Point Raceway in Sonoma, California, at the gateway to the California Wine Country. They have a full fleet of open-wheel formula racecars, performance sedans, and racing go-karts. They can help design custom driving experiences from a ½ day to multi-day program of racing, team building, seminars, golf, spas, wine tasting and dining.

If racing is not your thing, maybe you can learn about keeping a team on track by visiting a luxury resort or two.

Take a Cue from the Ritz-Carlton

For an example of how a large company keeps teams on track look no further than The Ritz-Carlton chain of luxury hotels.

The history of The Ritz-Carlton originates with The Ritz-Carlton, Boston. The standards of service, dining and facilities of this Boston landmark serve as a benchmark for all Ritz-Carlton hotels and resorts worldwide. In the early 1900s, several hotels were known as The Ritz-Carlton, in places such as Boston, Philadelphia, Pittsburgh, Atlantic City, New Jersey, and Boca Raton, Florida.

The legacy of The Ritz-Carlton, Boston begins with the celebrated hotelier Cesar Ritz, the "king of hoteliers and hotelier to kings." His philosophy of service and innovations redefined the luxury hotel experience in Europe through his management of The Ritz Paris and The Carlton in London. The Ritz-Carlton, Boston revolutionized hospitality in America by creating luxury in a hotel setting.

In 1998, the success of The Ritz-Carlton Hotel Company had attracted the attention of the hospitality industry, and the brand was purchased by Marriott International.

As you review this example, think about the ways you can build a genuine customer focus in your company.

Could you help keep your team on track by developing a credo? Here is the famous credo from the Ritz-Carlton:

The Ritz-Carlton Hotel is a place where the genuine care and comfort of our guests is our highest mission.

We pledge to provide the finest personal service and facilities for our guests who will always enjoy a warm, relaxed, yet refined ambience.

The Ritz-Carlton experience enlivens the senses, instills well-being, and fulfills even the unexpressed wishes and needs of our guests.

Service Values–I Am Proud to Be Ritz-Carlton

I build strong relationships and create Ritz-Carlton guests for life.

I am always responsive to the expressed and unexpressed wishes and needs of our guests.

I am empowered to create unique, memorable and personal experiences for our guests.

I understand my role in achieving the Key Success Factors, embracing Community Footprints and creating The Ritz-Carlton Mystique.

I continuously seek opportunities to innovate and improve The Ritz-Carlton experience.

I own and immediately resolve guest problems.

I create a work environment of teamwork and lateral service so that the needs of our guests and each other are met.

I have the opportunity to continuously learn and grow.

I am involved in the planning of the work that affects me.

I am proud of my professional appearance, language and behavior.

I protect the privacy and security of our guests, my fellow employees and the company's confidential information and assets.

I am responsible for uncompromising levels of cleanliness and creating a safe and accident-free environment.

The Employee Promise

At The Ritz-Carlton, our ladies and gentlemen are the most important resource in our service commitment to our guests.

By applying the principles of trust, honesty, respect, integrity and commitment, we nurture and maximize talent to the benefit of each individual and the company.

The Ritz-Carlton fosters a work environment where diversity is valued, quality of life is enhanced, individual aspirations are fulfilled, and The Ritz-Carlton Mystique is strengthened.

As you review this example, think about the ways you can keep your team on track by building a genuine customer focus in your company.

What Do You and Your Team Expect From Each Other?

What do you expect in your life? Expectations are important for keeping a team on track.

Do you find that you feel disappointed or angry, and you are not sure why? Well, you probably had an expectation that wasn't fulfilled. Expectations play a big part in our lives. Our expectations determine whether we feel good or bad—happy or sad—content or angry—over what happens in daily life. They impact how we feel about our relationships, work, friends, and people we meet on the street, special days like holidays or birthdays and the world around us.

Expectations set up the judge and jury on how we feel about our lives and ourselves. We give a great deal of power to our expectations! That is not to say that if we don't get what we expect that we shouldn't feel sad or mad. Yet, if we know more about our expectations and where they come from, then we can find ways to deal with them in a healthy manner. Then we can take our power back and have more choice in how we view and interact with our world. Please consider the following aspects of expectations when it comes to keeping a team on track.

So, how do expectations work? Well, first we gather and accept our expectations from a variety of sources, starting from a very young age. We learn much of our expectations from our families, which can include what to expect of others and ourselves, how feelings should be expressed, and how problems should be handled. If we learned from our family that people could not be trusted, then that plays into our expectations of the world around us.

Other expectations come from our religious beliefs (or those we have been brought up with), what we see in the media—television, movies, magazines, etc., and what our society and culture holds as valuable and important. These factors all impact different aspects of our lives, like how we expect to raise our children or relate in our relationships. Or what we expect to do in our careers or believe of our limitations and responsibilities. An example of this is how media gives us definite and perhaps narrow views of gender, which influences what we expect from men and women.

The next step is how our expectations are met or not met, and we have many unhealthy ways to try to meet them. Many struggle to fulfill them by pushing or controlling situations to fit into the mold already created. We may use manipulation, persuasion, passive aggression or intimidation (with anger or tears) to fill our expectations. Or we might not do anything and allow ourselves to be disappointed, so as to reinforce what we already believe about others or ourselves. When our expectations are not taken care of, then we feel those around us have failed us and that leads to anger and bitterness. We may feel used, abused and betrayed by others, which feeds into rage and distrust. Underneath the anger and betrayal is the feeling of not being loved and accepted by others and that really hurts. These feelings are made even stronger by memories of similar experiences from our past—times when we had disappointments with our parents, siblings, friends, teachers and others, when we may have felt unloved or rejected by those around us. This can even drive us to set up expectations of others, to gain what we feel we didn't receive as a child.

There are many different types of expectations that are based on looking to others for approval, respect, attention, and love; validation of our good self, qualities and success; to have control or power in situations; to be taken care of by others and so on. If we didn't receive this when growing up then that would impact our expectations of whether or not we might achieve these now. We may even unconsciously select or attract people to fill these types of expectations, who may not be able to do so.

So, we sabotage ourselves and create failure from the very beginning. We may choose people that have similar issues to those from our past, like someone who has a similar temperament to our father or mother. That means we are recreating the past with all the old expectations in an effort to resolve old issues. These situations will keep coming up until we are ready to heal them. For example, many people seem to have, time after time—job after job, similar problems with their supervisors or coworkers. They need to trace the issues back to the original source and work them out there before dealing with the present issues.

When we can understand our expectations and where they come from, then we can begin to select those we wish to keep and begin to resolve those that hold us back. We begin to gain more control and feel more satisfied with our lives. Expectations can bring hope, excitement and profitability to our team and into the entire organization. We just need to be sure that we are directing, not following, them in our lives.

Team Building Code Crackers

A few tips on handling expectations to keep your team on track:

Managing Expectations. It helps to be aware of what you expect, and disappointment is your first clue that an expectation was unfulfilled. Ask yourself what did you expect? What were you looking for in this situation or this person? You might need to dig around some to get to the primary issue.

Evaluating Expectations. Next, it is important to evaluate whether or not your expectation was reasonable and realistic. Many times, we have expectations that are not reasonable or realistic, but that doesn't mean that we are "bad" or demanding. It just means that we hope for things that, perhaps, we didn't get at some time in our life. Occasionally, I find myself expecting my husband to know something I want or need without him being informed of my desires. What I am doing is wanting him to read my mind, which might be connected to my past where I didn't always feel emotionally attended to. Acting on unreasonable or unrealistic expectations can cause intense disappointment and conflict with others. When evaluating your expectations, be honest with yourself—is your expectation reasonable and realistic? For example, expecting yourself to never get angry or sad is pretty unrealistic. Lastly, be clear what you expect with others. You must be able to express your expectations and not assume that others would or should know what you want. It's difficult to get your expectations filled if you can't communicate them to others.

Consider Influencing Factors. An exercise to help you explore your expectations is looking at various factors that impact them. For team members, you might want to consider what you are looking for, and what do you need/want from them. How do you expect to handle conflict and communication with them? Who has control and power in this relationship? Who makes decisions and what is expected around that? How are feelings and thoughts shared? How much trust do you have in your team member? How much do you rely on each other? How do you define forgiveness and how does that affect your work relationship? What experiences, beliefs and values are impacting your expectations with them? How do you approach problems and situations with your team members—as a team or independently and what does that do to your expectations?

Don't Forget Self-Expectations. We have many, many expectations that we place upon ourselves, which should also be explored. What do you expect of yourself? Do you expect yourself to be a certain way? Do you expect yourself to be perfect, good and controlled? Do you judge and criticize yourself when you can't be that way? Do you feel you should be taking care of others—perhaps filling their needs and desires before your own? Do you need to be in control and what do you expect of others? How do you handle conflict and why? Is it ok for you to be wrong or not know something? Do you believe that feelings must be handled in a certain way, like never losing one's temper? Where did all these expectations come from and why?

Notes:

www.lighthouseconsulting.com

Chapter 9

Twelve Resources for Tackling Team Building

One. Take a Systematic Approach. "Teamwork has never been easy—but in recent years it has become much more complex. And the trends that make it more difficult seem likely to continue, as teams become increasingly global, virtual, and project-driven. Taking a systematic approach to analyzing how well your team is set up to succeed—and identifying where improvements are needed—can make all the difference."

Martine Haas and Mark Mortenson, *Harvard Business Review*, "The Secrets of Great Teamwork" (June 2016)

Two. Communications is the Key. "A study from MIT's Human Dynamics Laboratory shows that when it comes to predicting the success of a great team, the most important element is how well the team communicates during informal meetings: With remarkable consistency, the data confirmed that communication indeed plays a critical role in building successful teams. In fact, we've found patterns of communication to be the most important predictor of a team's success. This doesn't mean team members have to be best friends outside of work, but managers should recognize that non-work discussions are critical to creating a team that looks out for each other. Otherwise, coworkers may begin to view one another as just cogs in the machine."

Gregory Ciotti, *Entrepreneur*, "10 Insights on Building, Motivating and Managing an Exceptional Team" (June 2014)

Three. Team Building Takes Great Leadership. "It takes great leadership to build great teams. Leaders who are not afraid to course correct, make the difficult decisions and establish standards of performance that are constantly being met—and improving at all times. Whether in the workplace, professional sports, or your local community, team building requires a keen understanding of people, their strengths and what gets them excited to work with others. Team building requires the management of egos and their constant demands for attention and recognition—not always warranted. Team building is both an art and a science and the leader who can consistently build high performance teams is worth their weight in gold."

Glenn Llopis, for Forbes.com (2012)

Four. Team Building Requires Trust. "Trust is a key factor in team building and a needed enabler for cooperation. In general, trust building is a slow process, but it can be accelerated with open interaction and good communication skills.… Existing research emphasizes the importance of trust and team building. Trust is a crucial factor for team performance (Erdem et al., 2003); without trust, team members are not willing to voice their opinions, questions, and improvement ideas. Also, team members do not display their feelings and they are not willing to help others (Sitkin and Roth, 1993; Jones and George, 1998). All these aspects are crucial in cocreation of business networks and in the building of high-performing teams. The preliminary results of our study reinforce the insights from the literature and contribute further insights relating to trust in high-performing teams and within business ecosystems. In particularly, these results highlight the importance of sharing critical information and having a high level of communication through constant interaction."

Mila Hakanen and Aki Soudunsaari, *Technology Innovation Management Review*, "Building Trust in High-Performing Teams" (June 2012)

Five. Get the Resources Necessary for Success. "The lesson we are working hard on learning here is not to accept responsibility or promise an outcome unless you have the necessary resources and support to deliver on your promise. Being heroic or a martyr will only get you crucified in the end, will allow others to be delusional about getting the desired outcomes until after the deadline has passed and you have failed, or until you collapse or explode in frustration. Develop a checklist or process for yourself that allows you to be rigorous about the resources and time you need, the support you need from others, and any authorizations that must come from others before you say yes. Face any limiting beliefs you have about being able to be direct and sensitive about the subject, and communicate until you are clear that you can perform."

Dwight Frindt, Vistage Chair, principal and co-founder of 2130 Partners

Six. Recruit for Initiative. "Who do you have on your team that demonstrates initiative? What if you could get another one or two? You've probably come to recognize that the ones with initiative exceed your expectations, frequently go above and beyond, and get more done in a single day than the majority of their peers. Measuring initiative is actually quite easy. Initiative is a life-long pattern of behavior. You don't wake up at thirteen, twenty-five, thirty-two or forty-seven years old and suddenly declare that you're going to be proactive for the rest of your life. The candidates who have it will share example after example with you in the interview. The ones who don't—they'll struggle to come up with a few substantive examples."

Barry Deutsch, partner and executive co-author of *You're Not the Person I Hired*

Seven. Be a Consistent and Predictable Leader. "Don't worry about your people seeing you as some 'perfect' leader. Don't get too caught up in what appearance they might find attractive or what message they might like to hear. In that sense, be true to yourself. But also realize that you cast a large wake of influence over every person in the company. And the consistency of that influence brings stability to the organization. Many times a day, decisions are being made on your behalf. Can your people predict what decision you would make? Do they know how you would react to certain situations? Is it evident from their numerous interactions with you what you stand for, what you won't tolerate, and what you believe are the keys to our success? Do they know what decisions you don't care about, which ones you want to be informed about, which ones you want to participate in, and which ones you want to make yourself? If so, you are consistent and predictable. And, those who work for you will find it easy to know what to do in most every situation they face."

Mark Murphy, Vistage chair in Orange County, California

Eight. Team Building is an Investment that Pays Dividends. "Despite its reputation for being, well, lame, team building is the most important investment you can make for your people. It builds trust, mitigates conflict, encourages communication, and increases collaboration. Effective team building means more engaged employees, which is good for company culture and boosting the bottom line. It can also be adventurous and enjoyable if you do it with a little pizzazz."

Brian Scudamore, founder and CEO of O2E Brands, for Forbes.com

Nine. Study After Study Proves that Team Building Matters. "Thirty-six published studies of an organization development strategy, team building, were reviewed…Team building appears to be an intervention with great potential for improving employee attitudes, perceptions, and behaviors as well as organizational effectiveness."

Kenneth P. De Meuse and S. Jay Liebowitz, *Sage Journals*, An Empirical Analysis of Team-Building Research (September 1, 1981)

Ten. Stress the Bigger Picture. "People in every workplace talk about building the team, working as a team, and my team, but few understand how to create the experience of team work or how to develop an effective team. Belonging to a team, in the broadest sense, is a result of feeling part of something larger than yourself. It has a lot to do with your understanding of the mission or objectives of your organization. In a team-oriented environment, you contribute to the overall success of the organization. You work with fellow members of the organization to produce these results. Even though you have a specific job function and you belong to a specific department, you are unified with other organization members to accomplish the overall objectives. The bigger picture drives your actions; your function exists to serve the bigger picture."

Susan M. Heathfield, *Your Guide to Human Resources* (2007)

Eleven. Team Building Improves Satisfaction and Retention. "A series of team-building activities were conducted on a medical-surgical unit and their impact on staff's communication and job satisfaction was examined. Forty-four unit personnel participated in the interventions. Staff communication and job satisfaction were measured before and after the intervention. The findings linked team-building activities with improved staff communication and job satisfaction. Team-building strategies assisted the nurse leader/manager to build an effective work team by strengthening communication and interpersonal relationships so that the staff could function as a more cohesive group."

Mary Anne Amos, Jie Hu, and Charlotte A. Herrick, *Journal for Nurses in Staff Development,* "The Impact of Team Building on Communication and Job Satisfaction of Nursing Staff" (2005).

Twelve. Team Building Helps Across the Board. "Our study considers the impact of four specific team-building components (goal setting, interpersonal relations, problem solving, and role clarification) on cognitive, affective, process, and performance outcomes. Results (based on 60 correlations) suggest that team building has a positive moderate effect across all team outcomes. In terms of specific outcomes, team building was most strongly related to affective and process outcomes. Results are also presented on the differential effectiveness of team building based upon the team size."

Cameron Klein, Deborah Diaz Granados, Eduardo Salas, et al, *Sage Journals*, "Does Team Building Work?" (January 16, 2009)

Notes:

www.lighthouseconsulting.com

Chapter 10

Tips and Tactics for High Performance

In closing, we wanted to end the book sharing some insights from a few of the wisest people we know when it comes to turbo-charging high-performance teams. Allow us to introduce these remarkable advisors and let them share in their own words how to lead for high performance.

Creating Healthy High-Performance Teams

Paul David Walker is a nationally recognized author and trusted advisor to the CEOs of mid-sized and Fortune 500 companies. Walker is known for blending a practical, business-minded world view with the vision of a philosopher trained by some of the most profound business leaders and spiritual teachers of our time.

He has uncovered proven strategies to impact immediate and long-term results, create accountable action teams, and develop a position of strength in the marketplace. Here are his thoughts on building healthy high-performance teams:

> *A healthy high-performance team is committed to each other's success and the success of the mission and the business. When the New England Patriots overcame a twenty-five-point deficit to take the game into overtime and win 34-28 over the Atlanta Falcons in the 2017 Super Bowl, and executed the greatest comeback in NFL Super Bowl history, the reporters asked how they did it.*
>
> *Tom Brady, the quarterback, said, "We all brought each other back."*
>
> *Coach Bill Belichick said, "We love each other."*
>
> *Coach Belichick always says, "On a team, it's not the strength of the individual players, but it is the strength of the unit and how they all function together."*
>
> *Business and organizational teams could work together the same way. I have spent the last thirty years building healthy high-*

performance teams of business leaders. The challenge is that the insights that Tom Brady and Bill Belichick shared are not as obvious for business teams. In football everyone has a specific talent that fits a position on the team: quarterback, wide receiver, linebacker. On business teams, individuals are always trying to move up, and leading a business team is much more complex. The following describes how I do that.

The first step in becoming a team committed to each other's success is to know each person's strengths, weaknesses and potential. Each member of the team is committed to helping unleash each team player's potential, the potential of the team, and business. This creates a safe field for innovation and exploration. Each understands and has expertise in their roles, and those roles synchronize to form a team ready to build on insight and act upon opportunities uncovered. This is a healthy high-performance team.

Getting Senior Leadership to Operate as a High-Performance Team

In his relentless effort to deliver uncommon results, Steven L. Phillips, Ph.D., has built an enviable reputation for his senior team consulting, focusing on senior leadership off-sites that get results. His proven strategy of simultaneously focusing on both strategic planning and high-performance team development offers powerful and long-lasting results.

Dr. Phillips is a sought-after speaker for conferences and organizations worldwide. He has helped thousands of individuals and organizations establish new levels of teamwork, transformation, and performance, all specifically targeted toward bottom line results. Here is his advice on creating high performance leadership:

Senior leadership must not only create their strategic and operating plans together, they must operate as a high-performance team. This is not as easy as it sounds. The short cut is to work on the team dynamics while in the yearly planning process. Then, every quarter, meet as a team for an afternoon, adjust strategy as appropriate, and keep the team in tip top condition. Building this habit will ensure the company and the senior team will thrive.

Here are a few of Steve's adages for creating high performance teams:

- "It is much easier to maintain high performance than it is to get there in the first place."

- "For senior leaders to drive their company forward, they not only need to be competent in their craft and as leaders, but they must operate with each other as a high-performance team."

- "The hidden secret of high-performance teams is process discipline."

- "Teams not only lose great productivity when they are not disciplined with processes but they also lose all chance to become truly high performance. Lack of process discipline is the hidden killer of high-performance teams."

Go Offsite to Unlock the Power of the Team

Mark Lefko once purchased twenty-five companies in twenty-nine months as an investment banker. Today he serves as CEO of the Lefko Group, a corporate retreat and facilitation company headquartered in California. Lefko Group provides services to companies in metropolitan or remote locations, and even internationally.

Lefko's business expertise is extensive. His background includes seven years as a CPA with Arthur Andersen, four years as CFO of a $6 billion mortgage company, nine years as an investment banker, and two years as a Chairman at TEC Worldwide (now Vistage, the International CEO membership organization). Here are his thoughts on unlocking the power of the team:

The terms "team," "teamwork," and "team spirit" are much bandied about in the management literature, but how exactly do you unlock the power of a team? Given effective planning and facilitation, off-site retreats are a sure way to do so. Why?

In the daily race of the office environment, everyone is heavily focused on the tactical. Huge amounts of information, multitasking and frequent change of direction make strategic thinking and planning next to impossible. It's an environment that discourages consistent communication and leaves little room for creativity.

At a retreat, on the other hand, people can interact without distraction. They can concentrate on working on the business rather than in the business. There is time and space for in-depth thinking and communication. This focused interaction in turn deepens the relationships between colleagues and their mutual understanding of goals and values.

Retreats are a safe environment in which to freewheel about future possibilities, brainstorm about new products and services, and build consensus around ideas and priorities.

The Secret Sauce of High Performance

Larry Cassidy has participated with chief executives in over 13,000 coaching discussions regarding all aspects of their businesses, including creating high-performance teams. Cassidy has been a group chair with Vistage for almost thirty-one years and works monthly with almost fifty Southern California executives in two chief executive groups and one group of key executives. In 2018 he facilitated his 1,500th Vistage meeting. He has received multiple Chair Excellence Awards from Vistage and the coveted Don Cope Award, the highest recognition accorded chairs for dedication and excellence in exemplifying Vistage's mission and core values.

Cassidy has five criteria for teammates that he teaches business leaders:

1. *I want people who "get it." Every job of substance has one or two things that you have to fundamentally get.*
2. *I want people who are "all in." These are people who are committed to bringing their A-game, ones who are driven to bring the best they have.*

3. *I want people who do "the right thing." This is about choosing doing right over wrong every time.*
4. *I want people you can "count on." When they say they do something, you know it will be done.*
5. *I want people who I want to "hang out with." These are people who are just plain enjoyable to be around.*

When you find team members like that, what is the leader's job? Here are Cassidy's thoughts:

1. *The leader must establish and sell the vision. Great people want to know the target.*
2. *The leader must establish the core values of the firm. Not only that, the leader must make the values clear to all.*
3. *The leader must get the right people doing the right assignments (to paraphrase Jim Collins, the right people on the bus in the right seats).*
4. *The leader must develop an effective, scalable strategy.*
5. *The leader must remove the obstacles, roadblocks, and barriers. The team needs room to run.*
6. *The leader must provide the resources the team needs. Even the greatest sportscar in the world won't go anywhere without gas.*
7. *The leader must adjust things when it isn't working. It does not matter whose idea it was. If it isn't working, stop doing it.*

Getting Teams Engaged for High Performance

Tony Mulkern specializes in the development and delivery of leading-edge executive coaching, executive launch and leadership development programs, especially in the financial services and technology sectors. He is founder and president of Mulkern Associates, a Los Angeles-based consulting services firm.

Here is advice from Mulkern:

Numerous surveys have shown that only about 21 percent of workers are fully engaged, 71 percent are partially engaged, and 8 percent are fully disengaged. And these numbers reflect the general situation in good times.

If only 21 percent are fully exerting themselves at the oars, and nearly 10 percent are just going for a ride, your ship is in trouble, especially when another ship—the competition—is chasing you.

To save the term "employee engagement" from becoming one more vague business cliché, it is worth looking at its original meaning. It contains four elements:

- *A sense of urgency*
- *Feeling focused*
- *Feeling of intensity*
- *Enthusiasm*

Why is this important? The Gallup organization in 2009 estimated from their analysis of nearly 200,000 individuals from 8,000 companies that organizations with high levels of employee engagement can achieve the following:

- *12 percent higher customer satisfaction/loyalty*
- *18 percent more productivity*
- *12 percent greater profitability*

Other studies have shown similar results, plus the increased physical and psychological well-being of employees who are fully engaged.

So, what are some strategies for having a focused, enthusiastic, intensely energetic team show up every day with a sense of urgency?

In general, the team will be no more committed than the leaders. You set the high mark. When was the last time you did some self-reflection regarding your vision for the organization, thought about how it relates to your core values as a person, and expressed why your objectives and goals are worth pursuing, and what the future might hold once the winds fill your sails again? A disengaged crew indicates a disengaged or only partly engaged leadership.

When employees complain about not getting respect, as they often do, it is because they receive the benefit of too few of these listed behaviors. There is no need to belabor them in detail here, since most leaders who are readers know exactly what they are. Ask your colleagues—and especially your executive assistant if you are lucky enough to have one—how you could do more of these. Then follow at least some of their suggestions.

Some employees who are disengaged say that not much is asked or expected of them. Your job is to inspire outstanding performance and enthusiastic contributions—it is not to try to be popular. Research has shown that leaders who want above all to be liked rather than respected end up being neither respected nor liked. They are seen as gutless, inconsistent, and unfair.

One Last Thought from the Authors

We would love to hear from you on how you used the ideas in *Cracking the High-Performance Team Code*. Please share your thoughts with us by visiting our website at www.lighthouseconsulting.com. You can also sign up for our newsletter that provides monthly proactive articles and for our monthly Open Line web programs.

Notes:

Appendix

Resources from Lighthouse Consulting Services, LLC

If you liked this book, you'll love our website. It is a gateway to a plethora of useful information and helpful services for managers faced with the daily challenges of running a successful business. Just visit www.lighthouseconsulting.com to find content and programs for taking your business to the next level by elevating the performance of your employees. Here's what you can find there.

Publications and Events

Looking for the latest thinking on interpersonal communication, personnel management, and leadership? Look no further than our monthly newsletter, web conferences, and books.

- Keeping on Track Newsletter and Blog
- Open Line Web Conference Events
- *Cracking the Personality Code*
- *Cracking the Business Code*
- *Cracking the High-Performance Team Code*

In-Depth Work Style and Personality Assessments

With in-depth work style and personality assessment testing from LCS, you can quickly obtain objective information on a candidate's strengths and weaknesses, interview questions, and expert guidance on how best to manage that individual in your organization. Reduce the guesswork in hiring. Hire the right fit.

Skills Testing

How do you know for certain that a candidate has the right skills for the job? Smart managers rely on skills testing to aid their hiring decision process. View our catalog of on line tests for a range of office, professional, and technical jobs.

Talent Development Services

Elevating the performance of individuals and groups within your business is the key to company success. That's why LCS offers workshops and advisory services designed for results.

- Team Building Service
- Interpersonal Coaching Service
- Sino-American Management Style Service
- Talent Development Workshops
- Outplacement

See www.lighthouseconsulting.com for more information and how to contact us directly.

About the Authors

One could say that Dana and Ellen Borowka have seen it all when it comes to personalities and direct relationship between personality and team performance. Having conducted and interpreted over 20,000 in-depth work style and personality assessments since 1994, the Borowkas have earned a reputation for in-depth insight that helps their clients hire the right people and manage them for exceptional team performance. This expertise has made the Borowkas sought-after speakers on the topics of employee and team performance. Their first book, *Cracking the Personality Code*, is regarded as a leading text on the subject of in-depth work style and personality assessments. Their second book, *Cracking the Business Code*, is hailed for its key ideas with specific actions steps from a variety of thought leaders. The Borowkas co-founded Lighthouse Consulting Services, LLC, in Santa Monica, CA in 1994 and today the firm works with organizations around the world to create high performance companies with engaged, fulfilled employees.

Dana Borowka, MA, CEO and co-founder of Lighthouse Consulting Services, LLC, brings over thirty years of experience in business consulting into every client engagement. He has an undergraduate degree in human behavior and a master's degree in clinical psychology. He speaks regularly to Vistage International and other CEO peer groups, corporations, associations, and trade organizations.

Ellen Borowka, MA, Senior Analyst and co-founder of Lighthouse Consulting Services, LLC, has an undergraduate degree in sociology and a master's degree in counseling psychology. Since 1994 she has worked tirelessly to refine the processes, external communications, and best practices that have earned for LCS a reputation for responsiveness and high customer satisfaction.

They provide programs to help companies increase executive and employee productivity and well-being. Their clients range from small startups to Fortune 500 firms.

Other Books by Dana and Ellen Borowka

Cracking the Personality Code

Cracking the Business Code

www.lighthouseconsulting.com

Notes: